101 EASY SOLOS FOR SAXOPHONE

MB21947

BY JOE MARONI

© 2010 BY MEL BAY PUBLICATIONS, INC., PACIFIC, MO 63069.
ALL RIGHTS RESERVED. INTERNATIONAL COPYRIGHT SECURED. B.M.I. MADE AND PRINTED IN U.S.A.
No part of this publication may be reproduced in whole or in part, or stored in a retrieval system, or transmitted in any form
or by any means, electronic, mechanical, photocopy, recording, or otherwise, without written permission of the publisher.

Visit us on the Web at www.melbay.com or www.billsmusicshelf.com

Introduction

    The purpose of this Saxophone songbook is to provide the beginning Saxophone player with a repertoire of 101 familiar and easy to play tunes written for Saxophone. All the songs are written specifically for Saxophone utilizing dynamics, expression markings, and articulations. Key signatures for the songs are in a comfortable range suitable for the beginning Saxophone player.

    This songbook is an ideal supplement to any elementary Saxophone Method book. Most of the songs are appropriate for performance at concerts, recitals, and contests. Private teachers will assign one or two of the songs from this book at each lesson. The songs will help the beginning Saxophone student to develop fingering technique, rhythm reading ability, and confidence.

Contents

A Mighty Fortress is Our God	4
Alma Mater	5
Abide With Me	5
America the Beautiful	6
The Yellow Rose of Texas	6
America	7
Lightly Row	7
Angels We Have Heard On High	8
Aura Lee	9
Band Boys March	10
Beautiful Isle of Somewhere	11
Billy Boy	12
Cody Dance	12
Brahms Hymn	13
Bringing In the Sheaves	14
Ode to Joy	14
Calypso	15
Camptown Races	16
Life	16
Chester	17
Cielito Lindo	18
Come Back To Sorrento	19
Down At the Station	20
Au Clair de la Lune	20
Down in the Valley	21
Marianne	21
Faith of our Fathers	22
Lovely Evening	22
Frere Jacques	23
Row, Row, Row Your Boat	23
Get Along Little Doggies	24
Go Tell It on the Mountain	25
God Rest Ye Merry Gentlemen	26
Greensleeves	27
Hand Me down My Walking Cane	28
Evening Hymn	28
Harvest Time	29
Theme from the Second Symphony	29
Home, Sweet Home	30
I Need Thee Every Hour	31
Just a Closer Walk with Thee	31
In the Good Old Summertime	32
In the Hour of Trial	33
O Day Full of Grace	33
The Victor's March	34
It Came Upon A Midnight Clear	35
O Come, O Come. Emmanuel	35
Jesus Loves Me	36
Sing a Song of Sixpence	36
Joy to the World	37
Blessed Assurance	37
Largo	38
Learning to Lean	39
Little Brown Jug	40
Hark! The Herald Angels Sing	40
Long, Long Ago	41
Oh Susanna	41
Looby-Loo	42
Yankee Doodle	42
Little Star	43
Do Lord	43
Lullaby	44
Good King Wenceslas	44
The Man on the Flying Trapeze	45
All Through the Night	45
Marine's Hymn	46
Michael Row the Boat Ashore	47
Up On the Housetop	47
My Bonnie	48
Nearer My God, To Thee	49
North Star March	50
O Christmas Tree	50
Old MacDonald Had a Farm	51
Jingle Bells	51
This Old Man	52
London Bridges	52
On Top of Old Smokey	53
Red River Valley	54
We Gather Together	54
Rockabye Your Baby	55
The First Noel	55
Sacred Song	56
Deck the Halls	56
Santa Lucia	57
She'll Be Coming Round the Mountain	58
Shortnin' Bread	59
The Sidewalks of New York	60
Southern Roses	61
Sweet Hour of Prayer	62
Peace and Joy	62
The Bell Carol	63
The More We Get Together	64
Nobody Knows the Trouble I've Seen	64
The Wayfaring Stranger	65
There is a Tavern in the Town	66
Mama Don't 'Low	66
What Can the Matter Be	67
Clementine	67
When the Saints Go Marching In	68
Green Grow the Lilacs	68
Whispering Hope	69

A Mighty Fortress Is Our God

Moderately   Hymn

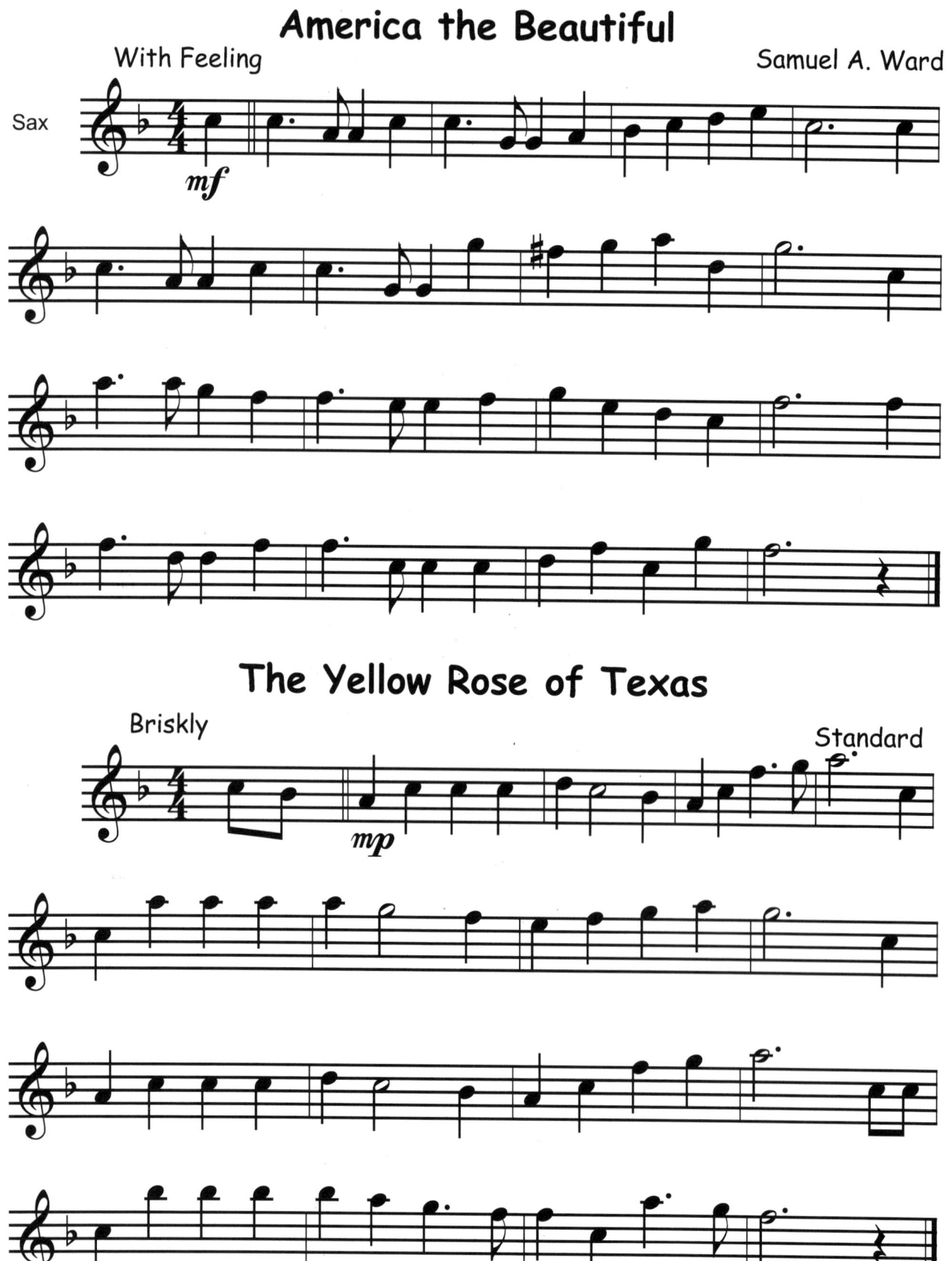

Angels We Have Heard On High

Aura Lee

Moderately Slow   Traditional

Band Boys March

Beautiful Isle Of Somewhere

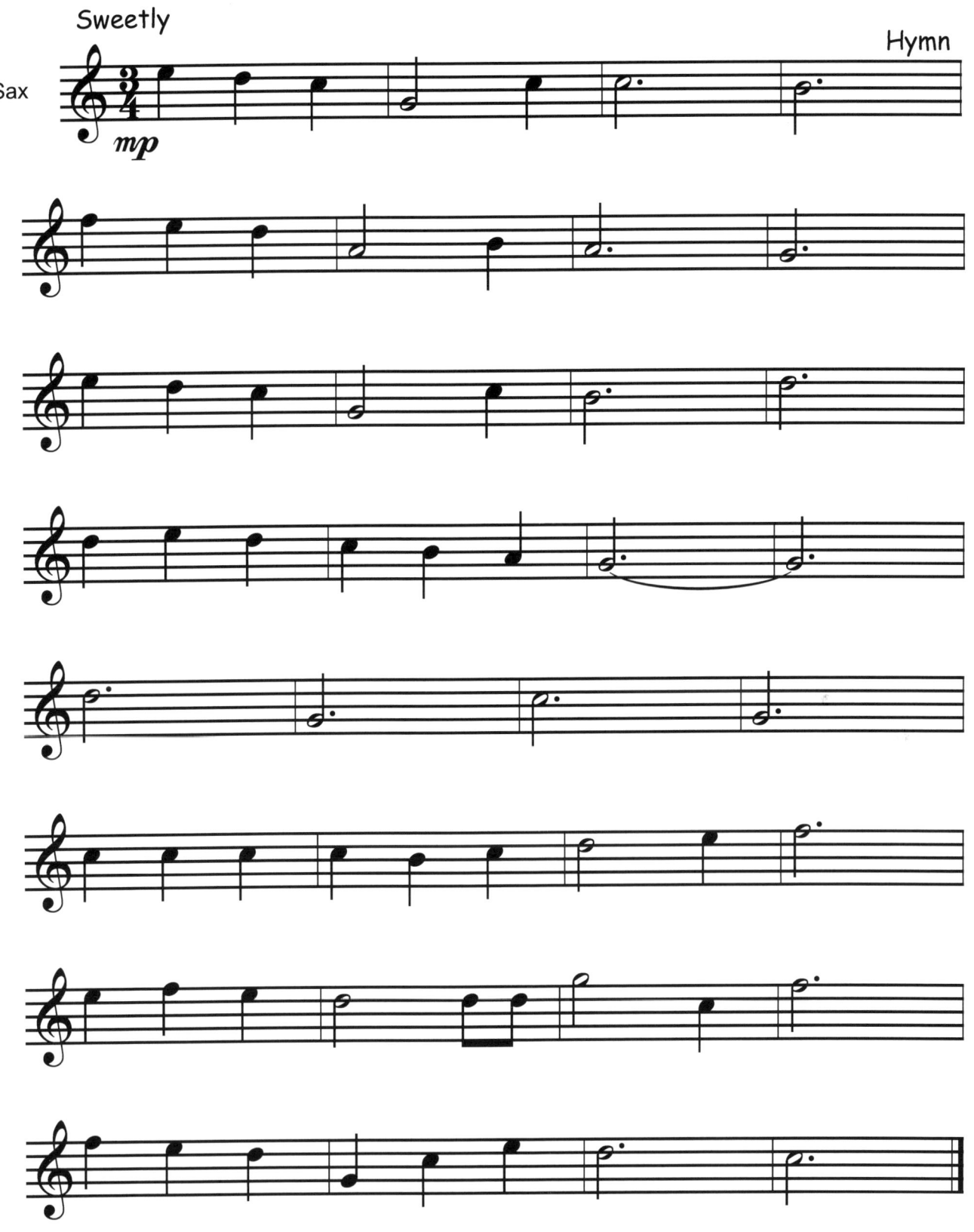

Brahms Lullaby

Calypso

With Calypso Beat

Ormont

Chester

William Billings

Cielito Lindo

Come Back To Sorrento

Italian Song

Down At The Station

Freely — Traditional

Au Clair de la Lune

Moderato — Lully

Down In the Valley

With Feeling   Standard

Sax.

mf

Marianne

Latin Feel   Latin

mp

Get Along Little Doggies

Country Swing
Cowboy Song

Go Tell It On The Mountain

African-American Spiritual

God Rest Ye Merry Gentlemen

Folk Dance-like 19th Century English Carol

Greensleeves

English Folk Song

Harvest Time

C. P. H.

Theme From the Second Symphony

P. J. Hayden

Home, Sweet Home

Slowly
Sicilian Air

I Need Thee Every Hour

Hymn

Just a Closer Walk With Thee

Hymn

In The Good Old Summertime

Slow Waltz   Standard

32

The Victor's March

School Song for the University of Michigan

Moderately — Sax. — *f* — March

It Came Upon A Midnight Clear

O Come, O Come. Emmanuel

Largo

Moderato Dvorak

Learning To Lean

Easy In One
Stalings

Little Brown Jug

Hark! The Herald Angles Sing

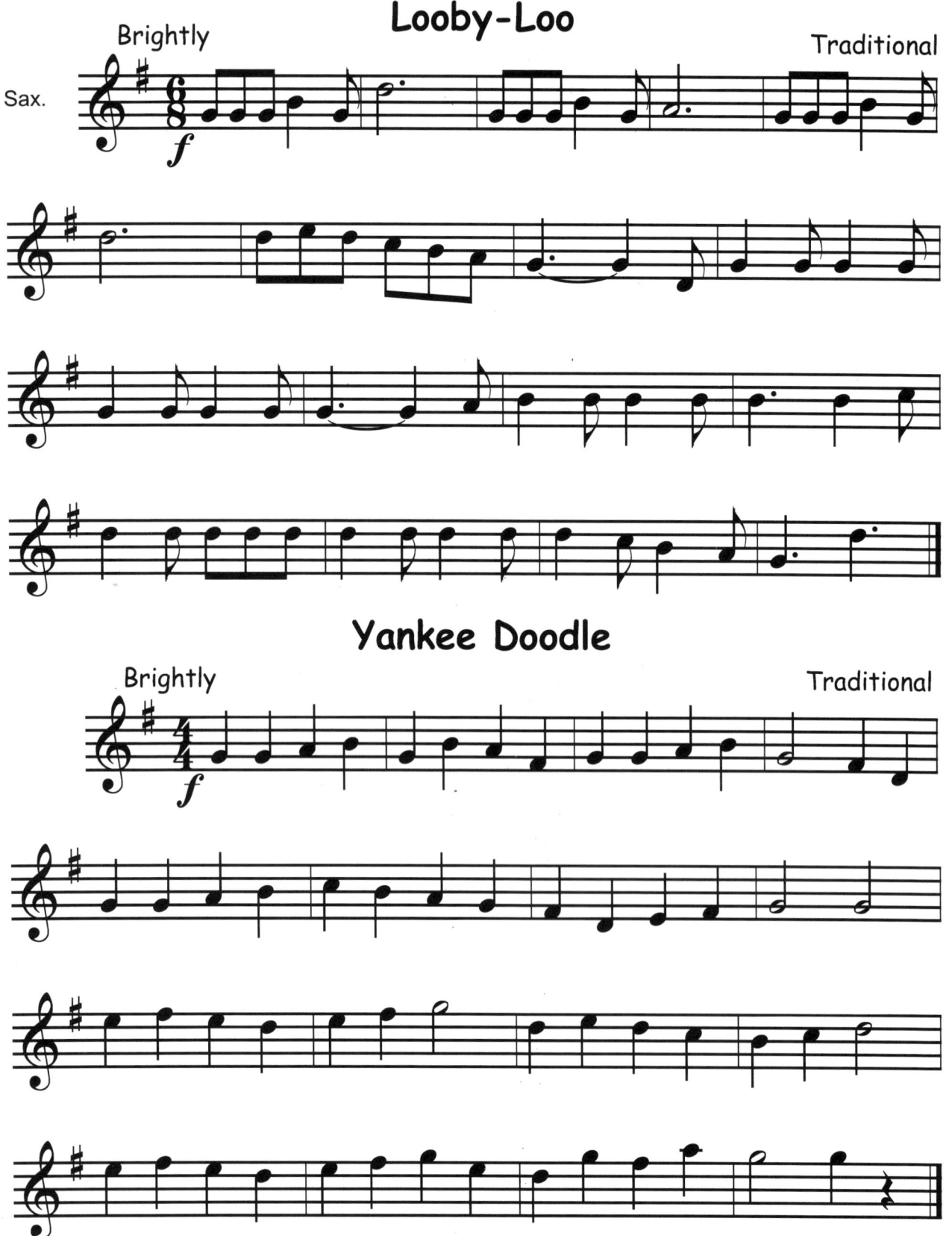

Little Star

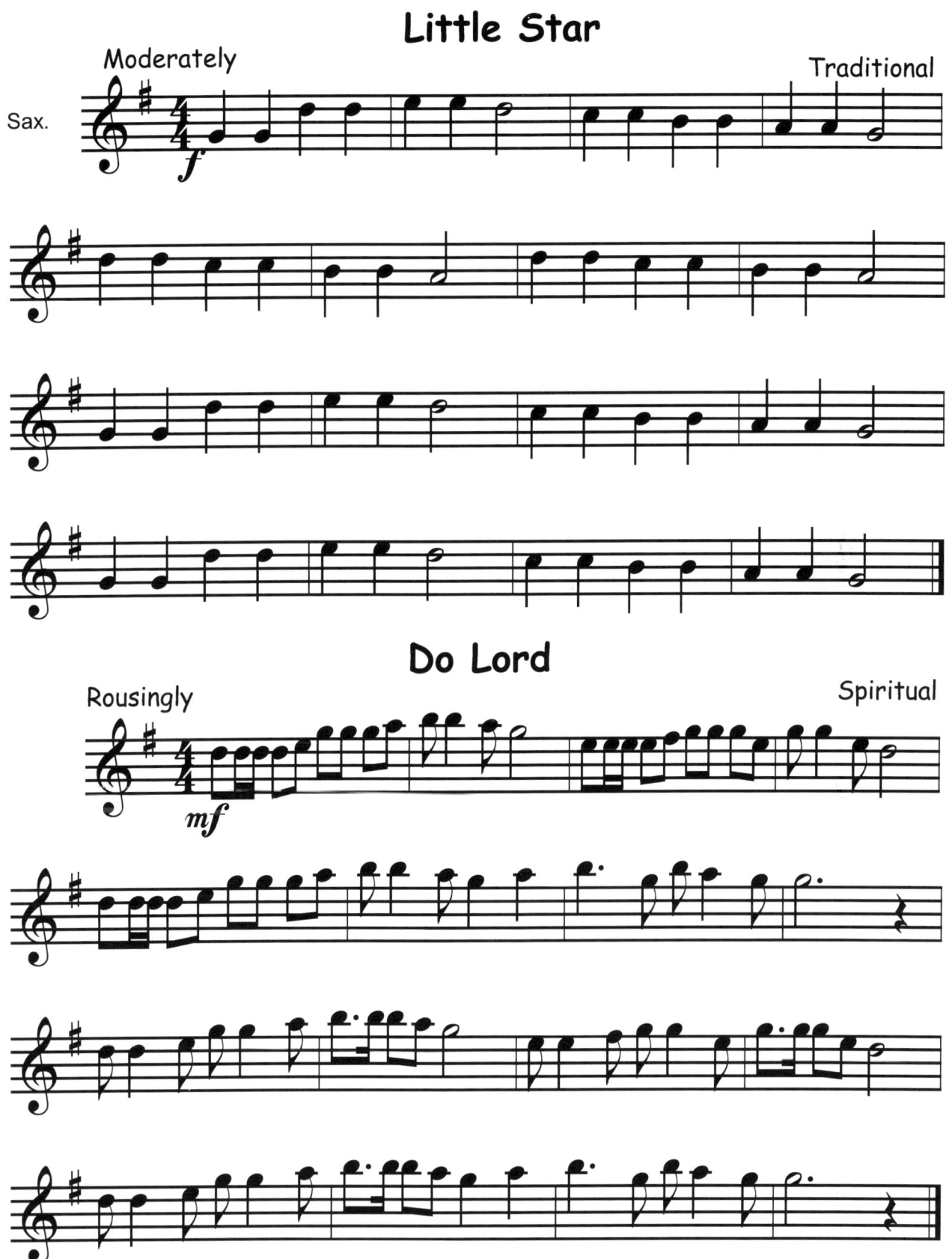

The Man On the Flying Trapeze

Brightly Traditional

Sax.

All Through the Night

Slowly Hymn

Marine's Hymn

March Traditional

Michael Row the Boat Ashore

Up On the Housetop

My Bonnie

Traditional

Nearer My God, To Thee

Hymn

North Star March

O Christmas Tree

Old MacDonald Had A Farm

On Top Of Old Smokey

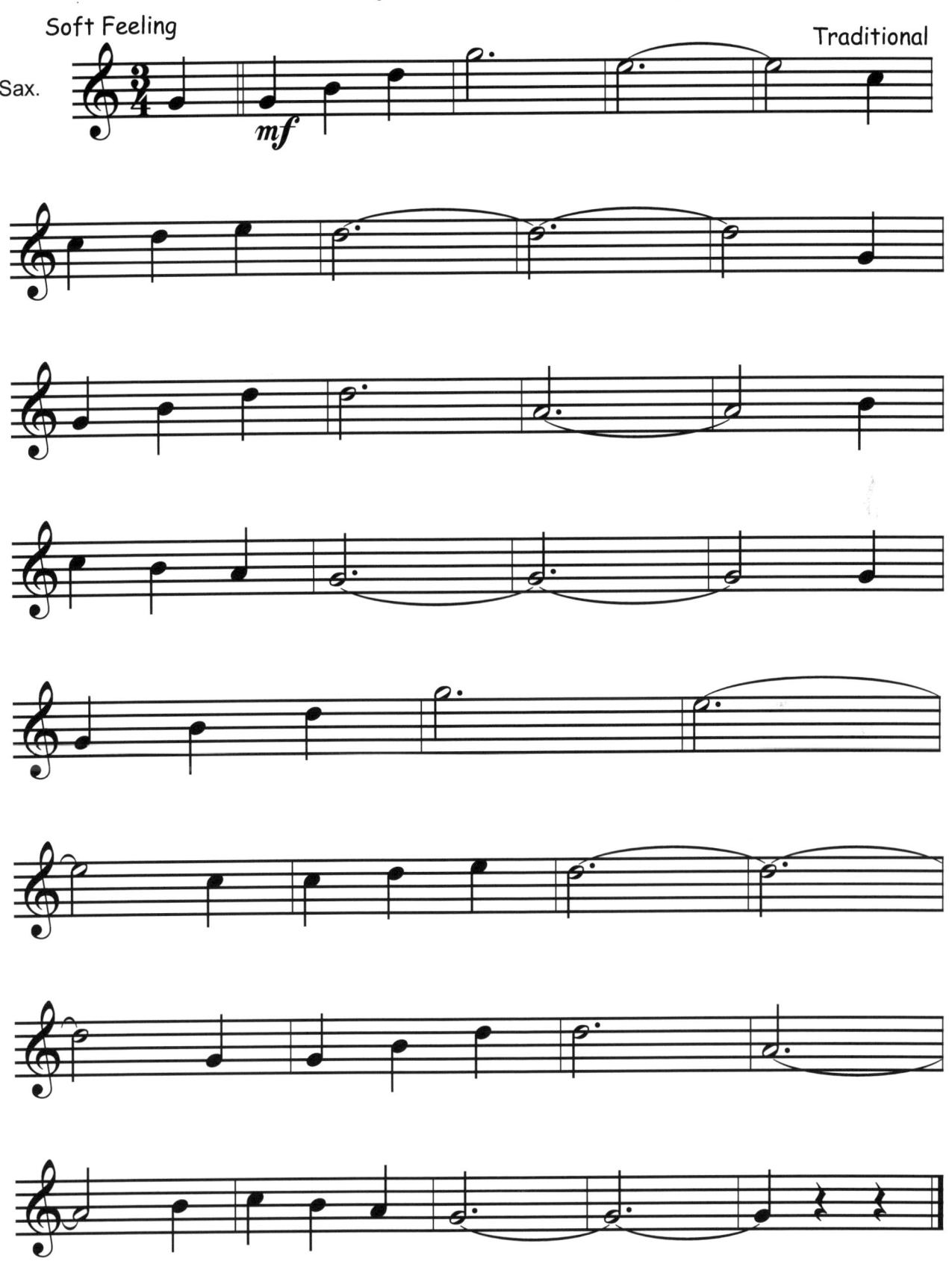

Santa Lucia

Easy Waltz Italian Standard

Sax.

mf

She'll be Coming Round the Mountain

Shortnin' Bread

The Sidewalks of New York

Waltz Tempo

Gay 90's

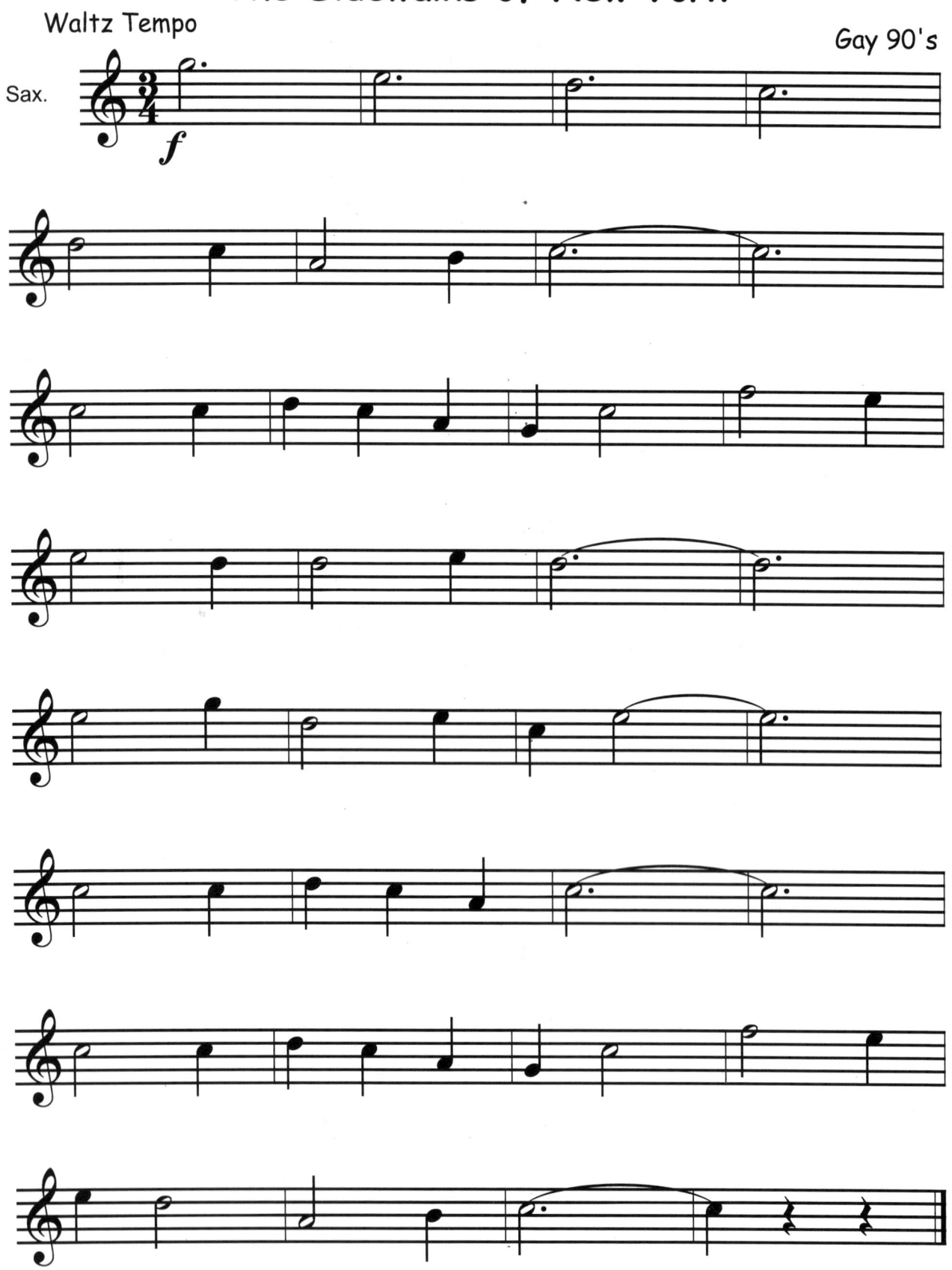

Southern Roses

Slow Waltz   Hymn

The Bell Carol

With Vigor
Traditional

The Wayfaring Stranger

Slowly   Traditional

There is a Tavern In the Town

Moderately — Traditional

Sax.

Mama Don't 'Low

Briskly — Traditional

What Can the Matter Be

Moderately　　　　　　　　　　　　　　　　　　　　　　　　　　　　Folk Song

Clementine

Lively　　　　　　　　　　　　　　　　　　　　　　　　　　　　Bluegrass Slong

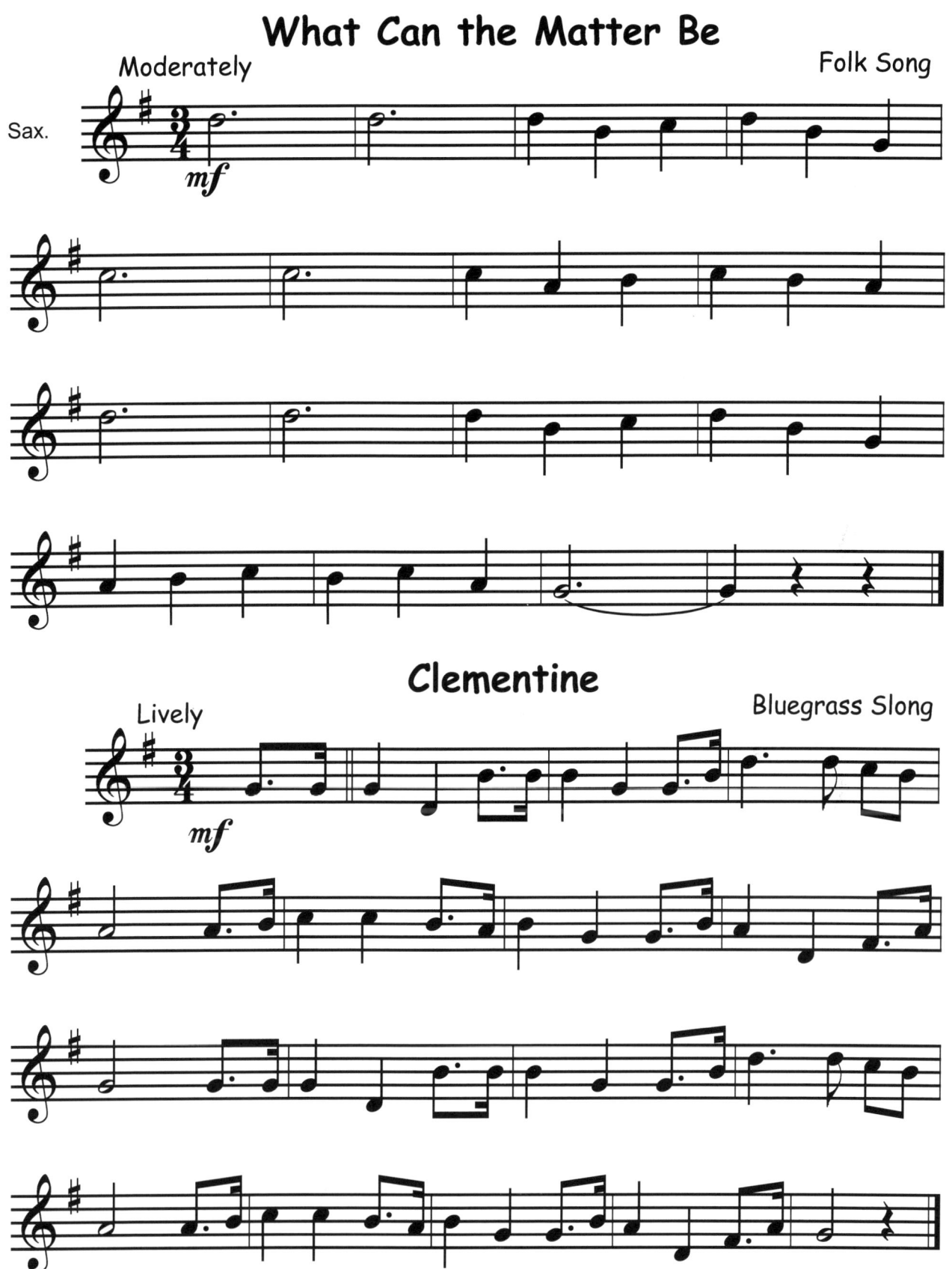

When the Saints Go Marching In

Whispering Hope

Gently, Lilting

Hymn

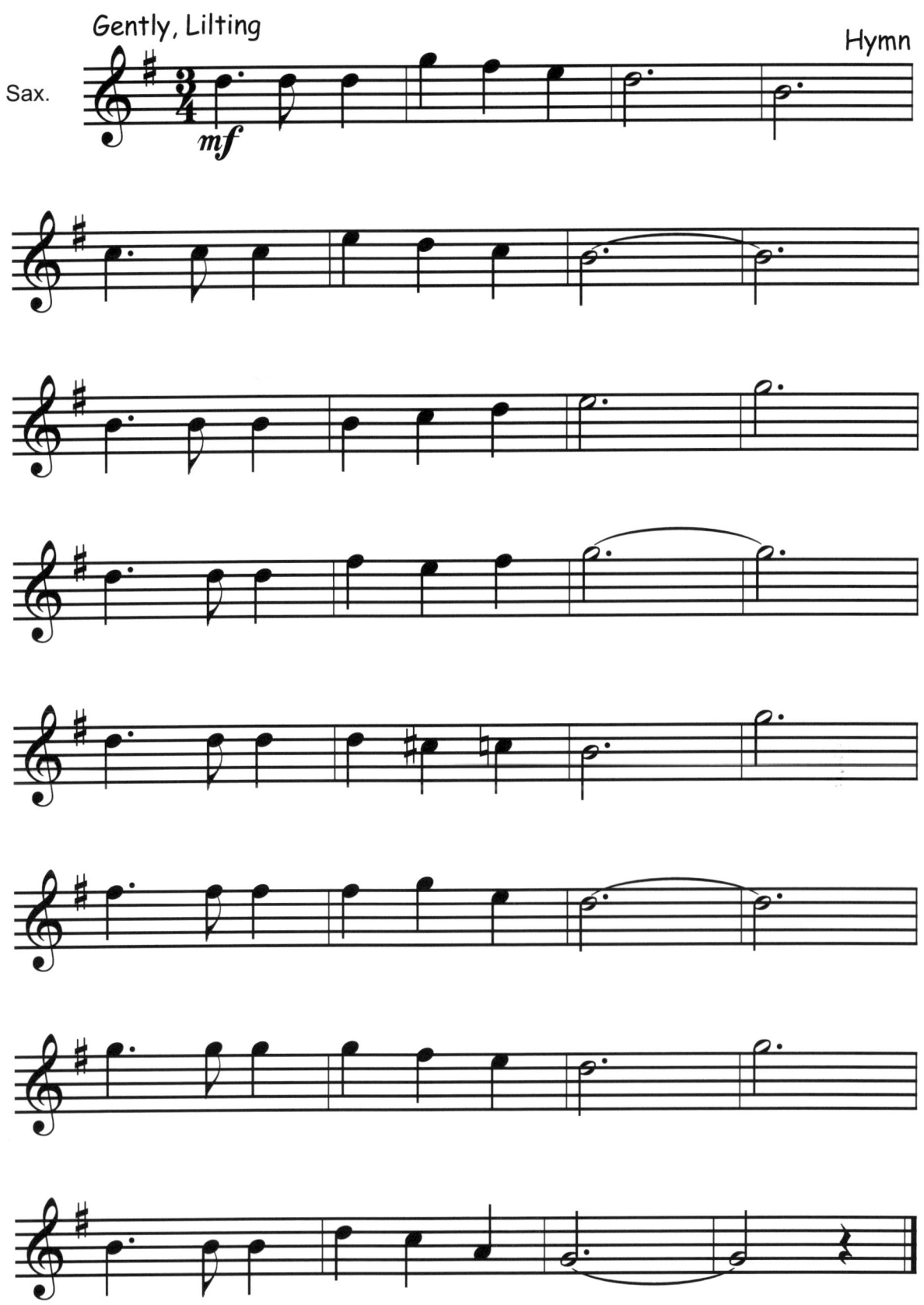

Joe Maroni

Other Saxophone Books by Joe Maroni

MB21809 Beginning Saxophone Songbook

Printed in Great Britain
by Amazon.co.uk, Ltd.,
Marston Gate.